"Mum, you Nutter!"

- Living with Bipolar

Disorder

Mary Clare

1. INTRODUCTION

Bipolar disorder is a mood disorder. It used to be called manic depression, which actually is probably more descriptive. Sometimes you are quite high and full of energy, (manic). Other times your mood becomes very low and leads to sinking into despair and depression.

There are two types. Bipolar I, which is more extreme and can cause hallucinations, disassociation from reality and dangerous behaviours due to feelings of invincibility and that nothing is impossible.

And Bipolar II, which is more common and causes extreme mood swings. Symptoms include talking too fast or too loud when manic. Also being full of energy, not needing much sleep, starting numerous projects, inability to sit still, constantly having to be doing *something.*

Your brain is racing. Thoughts coming so fast that your mouth cannot keep up. Ideas - usually in this state not very good ones – constantly bombarding your mind. You feel they are brilliant and must be acted on immediately. Like physical energy, the mental energy is boundless.

Then comes the depressive cycle. These last much longer. There is no energy. Getting out of bed can be the only goal achieved in the day, sometimes that is too much. To have a shower can use up an entire twenty four hours of energy. There are genuinely times when you consider if you can manage to turn over in bed - but decide against it. The effort involved at that stage is beyond reach.

Mentally, thoughts are sluggish. Both short, and long term, memory are poor. Trying to think is painful. Speaking becomes impossible.

Both physically and mentally there are two speeds. Go slow or stop.

I have Bipolar II, mixed with extreme anxiety disorder. This means as well as the above, I suffer panic attacks, agoraphobia, and night terrors, amongst other things.

The following is an account of how I've managed my life with various treatments, having varying amounts of success. From medication to Electro-Convulsive Therapy.

I hope it helps to know you're not alone.

2. THE GOOD, THE BAD AND THE UGLY – THERAPIES AND THERAPISTS

At the age of nineteen, when I had my first recognised 'breakdown' I unknowingly started on the long, slow, destination unknown, journey to various therapists to try various therapies.

I'd become more and more anxious at work. I was always a very nervous child and very introverted and shy teenager. I started to feel frightened and unable to cope, but felt this was stupid as there was nothing out of the ordinary for me to deal with. I'd been working for a couple of years in a normal, friendly, environment. Yet for the past few months I'd struggled to go in. There was no physical illness, just a gradual feeling of being overwhelmed. I'd never had a day off sick, but in the last few months I'd struggled to sleep, woke frequently through the night, lost my appetite and started to have regular panic attacks.

At first I managed to hide these by disappearing to the toilet when I started to shake so hard I spilt my coffee. Or pretending to have forgotten what I was going to say, when in fact I literally couldn't speak. I was paralysed with fear. Things became impossible when the vomiting started. There is only so long you can pretend to have eaten something that may have gone off, or picked up a bug that must be going round. It got to the stage where I was being sick throughout the night at the thought of facing going into work (even though I wasn't actually afraid of anything at work – it was so confusing). Then I was sick before I left for work, when I arrived at work and at various intervals during the day.

I carried on like this for months. Ever optimistic that whatever was wrong with me would eventually pass and life could carry on as normal. Eventually though I didn't make it as far as work and was sick on the train. The embarrassment was horrendous, and I felt so ashamed. I couldn't avoid the stares and disgusted looks and comments of other passengers, and as the train was moving, I couldn't escape them either. I cried throughout most of the day. I did not understand what was happening to me and I felt frightened and bewildered. I had put off seeing a doctor before because I didn't have a real (physical) problem. But even I had to accept I couldn't go through the rest of my life like this.

Okay, this was a long time ago, over thirty years now, but even for then, the advice was really crap! This was the first time in my life I had admitted to anyone that I thought I was going mad. I truly believed this at the time. Why else would I be in an inner screaming, outwardly frozen panic for no reason? The doctor listened to me, scribbled something in my notes and told me to go home and have a gin and take a few days off. Unbelievable now, but true. And at that time I thought doctors were Gods and their wisdom was not to be questioned. So I did exactly as he suggested. And actually, he was right! I felt great! The fear eased away completely for the first time in the best part of a year and the shaking stopped and I could eat again. Brilliant…for that evening. As I learned the hard way later, not something that can be relied on for a long term solution.

So I relaxed for a couple of days. Simply knowing I didn't have to do the journey really helped and I thought I'd cracked it and got better. Yes, I was that naïve. In my defence, I was still only a teenager. The following week I set off back to work and as I vomited all over the train platform in the height of an unexpected panic attack I realised this wasn't just going to go away. I changed from the train to the bus to get to and from work with the idea that if I felt I was going to be sick I could ring the bell and jump off. After needing to do this a couple of times and ending up in the middle of towns I didn't even recognise, I had to accept this wasn't going to work. I very unwillingly saw another doctor and was recommended to a psychologist. This was the first time I'd seen anyone in any capacity of a mental health worker, and he was really, really crap.

I went to the hospital for the appointment and followed the signs away from all the 'normal' departments to a large, dark, brick building set apart in the grounds. I pressed a buzzer and was let in and sent up to the top floor and told to wait on the chair outside the blue door. Eventually I heard singing coming from the bottom of the stairs which got louder and clearer as it came nearer.

Not humming, or a little catchy popular ditty, but top of the lungs, full strength opera. By the time the psychologist arrived in front of me (cowering in the chair trying to become invisible when he reached the top), he had his arms flung wide and seemed to want me to join in. I declined.

There then followed one of the strangest conversations I have ever had. Since then I have (unfortunately) had a lot of experience of how these things are supposed to go. This was my first time and I swore it would be my last. I felt obliged to stay for the consultation – in fact as I was still convinced I was insane I thought if I refused I would somehow be forced to be 'put away' in some asylum somewhere. Back then rights were never explained and I was definitely too shy to question whether I absolutely had to be there and answer all the questions. It didn't go well. There seemed to be a lot of questions about sex (even though he'd established early on in the conversation that I was a virgin). At the end of it he advised me to turn every churning in my stomach that signified the onset of a panic attack into a sexual feeling as they "both start the same way" and this would stop me actually being sick, and make the attack more enjoyable. I regret now keeping this to myself. God knows what this man said – or maybe even did? – to other young women. At the time I told my family and doctor he'd really helped, and I felt much better. I was terrified if I said anything other than that I'd be sent back for another session.

As I tried to hide the spiralling out of control feelings, I went into what I now realise was a deep depression. The anxiety I'd felt before had, I thought, been the worse thing a person could experience. The depression added to the anxiety managed to top it. As well as the symptoms I already had I now added a lethargy so strong some days I couldn't raise the strength to move. Where previously I'd managed on only four or five hours sleep a night during the week and caught up at weekends, now I could spend over twenty four hours without moving from bed. I couldn't see any point to living. There was no future for me as I'd had to give up work and all my future career dreams. I can best describe it as feeling that a heavy dark blanket had been put over me. So heavy that even to walk became an effort. I became silent too as talking seemed so pointless. Everything seemed black around me. Almost as though I was underground. Other people's voices seemed distant, and slightly muffled. I didn't want to commit suicide, but I absolutely didn't want to wake up anymore. I would go to sleep willing myself for this to be it, the last day over. Then I'd wake up and the tears would start because I was still here and still had to fight every minute.

I tried hypnotherapy. This was a very new idea in the nineteen eighties and there weren't many places that offered it. Unfortunately, there were also no such things as Google reviews to check just what sort of charlatan had set themselves up as a hypnotherapist either. I was taken for a ride by a very unscrupulous women who 'treated' me until I ran out of money (which didn't take long as I hadn't saved much when I was working).

She advertised in the local paper as using the latest and most effective way of treating people with phobias, addictions, anxiety, depression and eating disorders. I booked in and dragged myself out of the house to go and see her. I should have had my suspicions when she opened the door to her rented room in an unpopular area with a cigarette hanging out of her mouth and insisting she was always paid in cash.

The first session consisted of me signing some papers (no idea what, I was too ill to care at that stage). Then I sat on a chair in her 'office'. The office consisted of one room with a small coffee table and two chairs. There was a mini kitchen area in the corner with a kettle and tea things in it.

The supposed hypnotherapist sat me in one of the chairs, then put on a tape (I said it was a long time ago!). This was a relaxation tape that I subsequently found could be bought for a couple of pounds. The tape played for about three quarters of an hour during which time I was supposed to sit quietly and listen, and she took the other chair to the kitchen area, made herself a cup of tea, read magazines and smoked until the tape finished. At which point she took a lot of money – in cash – from me and said she'd see me again next week.

Unsurprisingly this didn't work very well. One week she even kept me waiting outside for nearly half an hour as she was "on the phone to someone who had real problems" – thanks. She then gave me the twenty minutes left, stopped the tape halfway through and still charged the full amount.

I know, I know. Everything's different with hindsight. But at the time I was neither well enough, nor mature enough to be able to deal with this in any other way than as I was told.

A few years pass and I have ups and downs. I can no longer manage to work in any sort of job with 'prospects', but when I was able to, I would do various jobs that I could manage for short periods of time.

During a more stable period I got married and moved into a tiny, old house with my husband which we did up between us. I was working part time and things were as normal as they could get for me when I fell into another massive depressive episode. Again, no reason. This is what makes the illness so hard. There is often no trigger, it just hits like a bolt from the blue and absolutely knocks you out.

I talk elsewhere about the different medications I have been put on, and I can't remember which was given for which episode for most of them – they are just another set of pills to me. But I do remember these as they were my first prescribed meds. I was put on 'Motipress'. The doctor said it was a drug designed for both anxiety and depression and she was sure it would cure me once and for all. Excellent! It was bright yellow and certainly looked impressive! (Which was as far as my knowledge went in those days).

Within weeks I had piled on so much weight none of my clothes fit me. Within a couple of months I had ballooned from a size ten to a size twenty. Psychologically that did me more damage than many of my other problems. It wasn't just heaviness. I was round! My body was alien to me, never mind anyone else. Friends and family were shocked when they saw me and tried very unsuccessfully to hide it. My face was a swollen circle. I went back to the doctor who assured me weight gain wasn't a side effect and it must be something else. Ironically nausea was another side effect (this one the doctor agreed with), but all the sickness didn't stop the weight piling on. I was given Stemetil to ease the sickness and told there must be another reason for the weight gain – but she had no idea what. (Of course it was the

Motipress, but again this was only recgonised years later).

When my size twenty clothes started to feel tight and I could no longer recognise myself in the mirror, and the fact that I was so different was making me feel so much worse I couldn't bear it. One day I picked up the pills and flushed every one of them down the toilet.

I didn't know then that you should never just stop taking medication you've been on for a long time and that you should gradually wean yourself off. I'd learned the hard was about side effects. I was now going to learn the hard way about withdrawal.

I started to feel very strange after a couple of days. My limbs felt 'fuzzy'. I felt as though I had ants crawling inside my body. I couldn't sleep, I was restless, the panic attacks came back with a vengeance. When I stood up, I was dizzy. My head ached and felt woolly. I couldn't think straight. My memory was ruined. I ached all over as though I had flu. I decided that this time I was actually dying. Wasn't sure what of, but definitely dying.

Now what do I do? I no longer trusted the medical profession. I certainly wasn't going to be put on any more tablets, seen by anymore 'weird' mental health professionals – private or public. I despaired. Then I had a brainwave. I remembered the doctor who'd suggested gin. That had definitely made me feel better. I wasn't a drinker, and didn't have any gin, but a glass of wine might help. It did. Then a couple. Soon I was having a couple of drinks every night. I found spirits worked even better! For the first time in my adult life I was going to bed without panicking and sleeping through. I may not feel great the next day, but so much better than having depression or swelling up with meds.

This went on for months. There was rarely a day that I didn't drink. I convinced myself it was fine as I never drank until the evening, even though I was getting through more and more as the weeks went on.

Then one day it didn't work anymore. The demons came back. I was used to alcohol now so maybe I

needed more? How could I be panicking again?
How could I be so scared I couldn't leave the house
again? I upped the drinking and it nearly killed me.

The anxiety was making me sick again, but
suddenly there was blood in it. I had been used to
my throat bleeding in the past from the almost
persistent vomiting at various stages in my life, but
this was different. There was quite a lot of blood
and it looked half digested. Then the pains began.
My stomach and back were in agony. I had tests
and found I had bleeding ulcers. I knew they
would be painful, but I'd never known pain like
this. Instead of easing, the pain gradually got
worse until it was excrutiating. I'm quite tough
with physical pain, but at the stage where I could
no longer sit, stand or lie without gasping we
called the doctor. He told me to take two

paracetamol and call him in the morning if I didn't feel better. By the time the morning came I was in hospital on a drip with my husband being told I may not make the night.

Apparently, the bleeding ulcers were the least of my problems. After months of drinking I had managed to give myself acute pancreatitis. The surgeons hadn't realised at first and while the blood tests were being done, before the results were back, I had already signed the pre-op form to have my gall bladder removed, as this was thought to be the problem. I was lucky to have one very good Consultant who looked at the blood results and asked some very good questions. He sent me for a scan which revealed a large pseudo cyst (an open, oozing cyst), on my pancreas. He then had a long chat with me and explained that it would be very difficult to operate on the cyst and – very frankly – that my weight would be an added risk, along with the complications of the bleeding ulcers and very poor general health. So instead I was told we'd wait and see and only operate if there was no alternative in a few days. I was then moved to the bed next to the nurses station, was told nil by mouth and left with a drip to deliver whatever was necessary.

The first few days I remember nothing but blood tests and various faces leaning over me. My parents, family members, husband. I remember waking up upside down a few times. Apparently when my blood pressure dropped so low that I passed out, the bed was tilted to turn me upside down, and when I came round again I was looking at the floor.

I had been nil by mouth for three or four days by then, and knew I must be improving when I was told I could have 5ml of water (a teaspoon) every hour to help my dry mouth. I was so excited! I clock watched the entire day. After a further two days I was allowed 10mls and the bed moved from beside the nurses station to one place further down. Gradually the amount of water was increased until one day I was moved much further down the ward and given a cup of tea. It was pale, overly sweet, weak, cold and disgusting. But it was the best drink I'd ever had! I then progressed to soup and eventually – after about three weeks - was able to get rid of the drip, which had been my unwanted constant companion, even pushed up to the curtain while I'd had a shower.

The day I was discharged the Consultant came back for a chat. He explained that my cyst was shrinking, and I'd have to come in for a couple more scans to make sure it had completely gone. That I had been 'unlucky' (that's one word for it!). That usually acute pancreatitis was only suffered by those who had been drinking excessively for many years. In fact it is apparently referred to as 'The old man's disease'. Poor old men. I wouldn't wish that pain on anyone.

I asked why I'd been moved all over the ward and he smiled but evaded the question. I found out later that my husband had asked the same thing and he'd explained that for the first few days they weren't sure I would make it and so I was placed closest to the nurses station so that I could be kept an eye on (and also, if the worst happened, discreetly moved out). I have no recollection or knowledge of this, but on the first or second night my husband and parents had been in to visit as they had been told they may not have another chance. As I improved my bed was moved further away and other patients moved nearer as necessary.

The Consultant finished our talk by explaining that I could never drink again (that was okay, knowing what it had done I didn't want to). Would have to watch the amount of fat in my diet for years to come, (Mmmm. Not too bad, I can manage that). Oh, and give up chocolate for about a year. What?! Forget it. No way. Not fair. No chocolate – at all? No. Ffs.

I may have moaned a little, but pain like that is a good incentive. I did as I was told. I measured every bit of fat I had and made sure daily it was never more than 10 grams for the first year, then gradually increased it. I have never touched alcohol since. I even gave up chocolate for one whole year – marked on the calendar to the day. Bloody Hell it was good!

My body recovered from both the effects of the medication and my own attempts to cure myself with alcohol, and I went back to a normal and healthy (for me) size twelve. Where I stayed, until two years later when I discovered to my absolute delight, that I was pregnant.

3. EARLY MOTHERHOOD

Two weeks overdue, early on a Monday morning, the day I was supposed to be induced, I gave birth to my first child. A beautiful baby girl. I'd had my waters broken after being two weeks late, and two days of back labour. Due, I discovered later to her facing the wrong way. "But she wasn't breech?" I queried with the midwife. "No love, what we call here 'face to pubes'". Mmm. Lovely.

Even then she was quite happy to stay where she was and had to be dragged out with forceps.

She may have had white, scaly patches where she had slightly dry skin from being overcooked. She may have also had a small red dot of blood on her forehead from where they'd scratched her while overzealously breaking my waters. She may even have had a pointed purple head a bit like a mauve Smurf due to the forceps. But she was, I swear, the most beautiful baby ever born.

I fell in love with her immediately. I felt such euphoria when I first held her. The midwives said that elation was natural due to hormones and endorphins surging through my body, and it would fade. But it didn't.

Immediately after the birth I was starving. In those days (1990's), the – constantly changing – advice was not to allow a woman in labour to eat in case she needed an emergency caesarian section under anaesthetic. I'd eaten at home for the first, very slow, day of labour, but had had nothing in the last 24 hours. As I gave my daughter her first feed, which triggered the expelling of the placenta (sorry if that's too much information!), a nurse was dispatched to get me some tea and toast. A second nurse was looking at the placenta intently, and started whispering to the midwife in the corner of the room.

Just as a plate of hot buttered toast and a steaming cup of tea was wafted tantalizingly close, I was told not to eat anything just yet while a doctor just 'had a quick look'. It transpired that my placenta had started to break up and some had remained inside me. "Perhaps you'd better not eat just yet, in case you need a general to remove the rest", said a very helpful, not starving young doctor.

At this point the senior midwife came into the room to check how things were going. Baby happy suckling, mum on verge of passing out through dehydration and lack of food! She took the situation in at a glance. "For pity's sake. Give the woman some sustenance. She's had nothing to eat or drink for over a day, no sleep over a two day labour and is now using the reserves of her energy to feed a new baby." This woman was my new best friend. I reached out for the treats to find an empty cup and a plate with a few breadcrumbs. And a very abashed husband. "Well I thought you couldn't have it and I've had a hard night too...". I can only just laugh about that now.

For those wondering, the remaining placenta come out of its own accord after a few days breast feeding, which speeded up all sorts of helpful recovery. (Most importantly for my vanity the shrinking back of my stomach).

My daughter and I had an immediate strong bond. I felt so lucky. And I know this doesn't happen straight away for a lot of mothers. I was lucky not to have to struggle in that respect. I felt an overpowering love that I had never even imagined could exist. I think those around me were more cautious, worried that the happy bubble I was living in would burst. But it didn't. I needed no medication. I felt better than I had in my whole life – both physically and mentally. My world felt complete. I can honestly say the sleepless nights were a small price to pay for such an enormous joy.

When she was a toddler we decided we'd like a sibling for her. It had taken me a while to be prepared to have another child, not because I didn't want one, but because I was convinced I could never love anyone as much as I loved my little girl and I knew people who didn't have the bond we did. I was scared I'd have a child and not be able to have enough love for two.

That worry disappeared as soon as I became pregnant again. My daughter was two, and we were going to have a new addition to the family in seven months.

My first midwife appointment was booked in at twelve weeks, but I never made it. A week or so before I should have seen the midwife I started to bleed. I rang the doctors and they told me to go to straight to the hospital. It was late, and as we hadn't told anyone about the pregnancy yet, we took our little toddler with us and went to the accident and emergency department as we'd been advised.

I remember them insisting on doing a pregnancy test. And not being seen until it had come back positive. At this stage a very thoughtless medic asked if the pregnancy was planned?! What sort of bloody awful, tactless, hurtful question is that? Yes, it was very much planned. But if it hadn't been what difference would that have made? I was still miscarrying for God's sake.

I was put on a trolley with our two year old sitting at the end on one of those bright orange blankets that was covering me. She thought it was great. A ride through the corridors on a bed. Magical! That is the only part of the whole ordeal that can actual make me smile. The simple happiness pure innocence can bring.

When we arrived at the ward my husband and daughter went for a little walk while I was examined. The doctor was kindly and sympathetic. I was holding on to hope until the last possible minute. He could tell by my pleading look. "Well", he drew the word out slowly. "There's a lot of blood." "I know", I interjected, not wanting to hear any more. "But the test was still positive tonight, so that means I must still be pregnant, doesn't it?" He shook his head gently. "With the amount of blood you're losing, and at this early stage, I'm afraid it would take a miracle". I was told to go home and come back in a few days for an ultrasound scan.

Over the next few days there was so much blood loss and clotting I didn't need a scan to tell me my womb was empty. I went anyway. I was put in the ultrasound waiting room with all the expectant mothers, beaming at each other and leaving the scanning room clutching their black and white baby pictures. I stared at the wall and then the ceiling so that no-one would be able to see the tears building up. Someone must have noticed as a nurse bustled up and with enormous compassion took me into a side room. "You shouldn't have been left to sit in there. Someone should have realised. Stay here until you're called in."

I don't think that situation would happen nowadays. I think 'someone' would have realised it wasn't appropriate for a woman going through a miscarriage to be sitting in a room full of happy, expectant mothers (and fathers). Not appropriate for anyone actually. Someone silently weeping in the corner is going to put a bit of a damper on things all round.

As expected, the ultrasound showed nothing there. Some staff at that hospital, in that department, were amazing. Others really did need to go on 'some sort of course'. As the sonographer finished telling me there was no longer any life inside me she finished with; "If you go to reception they'll book you in for a D and C to make absolutely sure there's nothing left in case of infection."

That was the moment my few years of good mental health finally crumbled. I know people feel very differently about pregnancy and birth, viability, and many other issues. And I respect that. But to me, personally, that was my baby I'd been carrying and the callousness of the dismissal was the straw that broke me.

This was in the October. As I stopped being able to eat or keep anything down, the weight started once again to fall from me. Not a normal, healthy drop off, but a shedding so drastic that my bones started to stand out. I went to the doctor and was prescribed an anti-depressant. This had no effect and after six weeks I was referred to a Community Psychiatric Unit day care centre for what I thought was personal help. I couldn't have been more wrong. This was the place nightmares were made.

I was met at the desk by a heavily tattooed, frightening (to me) man that we would locally have referred to as a 'brick shit house'. He seemed to take pleasure in knowing he was an intimidating figure and actively encourage fear in others. He looked me up and down and asked: Had I ever attempted suicide? Did I self harm? Was I violent? What drugs had I ever used? Was I still taking any? Did I have any criminal convictions? Who was my social worker? And the list kept going.

I know now that I was very naïve and relatively innocent. I have never taken drugs not prescribed (that's just me. My parents would have beaten the crap out of me if I had and I wouldn't have had any idea of how to get hold of them if I'd wanted to!). The idea of me being a criminal was laughable. I have such anxiety that I would come out in a hot sweat if I thought I'd broken a law by accident. And as for suicide. My daughter was my whole world, that wasn't a consideration while ever she was in my life. That's why I needed to keep fighting to get better.

When I'd finished the grilling, double doors were unlocked and I was led into a common/games room. I don't mean to come across as precious in any way, but I really didn't belong there. And they all knew it. I'd been sent (whether intentionally – or more probably by sheer negligence) to a drug rehabilitation centre. It may well have been a Community Health Project, but it was definitely not for those with a nervous disposition. I was absolutely terrified. People hung around in mini groups. A few were at a shabby pool table arguing over who was allowed to play. Many were 'in-fighting' in their smaller groups. A lot were obviously so drugged up they wouldn't even remember being there. I'm not prone to being fanciful, and I have never suffered paranoia (most other things, maybe), but there was a definite feeling of menace in that room. I was actually really scared. As some of them surrounded me, laughing, whistling, pushing close in to me, or just plain staring, wanting money or cigarettes, I understood two things. Firstly, why the man who'd let me in cultivated an air of someone not to be messed with; and secondly, that I did not belong here.

Mental Health Services have improved since then. They still have a long way to go, but I don't think anyone now would be put in such a dangerous and provocative position. Provocative on both sides. They probably saw me as some middle class bitch who wouldn't know hardship if it jumped up and bit her. Those people in that centre really needed help, and should have it available and accessible when they needed it. Equally, those who need a different sort of help should be able to access appropriate help without everyone with any type of need being lumped together in a 'mental health, one size fits all' melting pot.

I struggled on through December. By now I was vomiting steadily as soon as I tried to eat anything. I tried sugary drinks in the hope that at least some would remain in my system even after I was sick. I found it almost impossible to get the energy to get out of bed. One day slipped into another without differentiation. I had no idea if it was day or night. I had rolling panic attacks, very little sleep, always waking up with a bang in my head which preceded the next attack. I shook constantly, my hands unable to hold anything and my legs twitching and thrashing of their own accord.

On Christmas Eve I filled my daughter's stocking, paced all night and morning, threw Christmas dinner in the oven and went to bed. I didn't move from there for days other than to go to the toilet or throw up in the bucket by the bed.

I lost hope. I was a shit mother. A shit wife. I couldn't even stand up, and every pill seemed to be making me worse not better.

I didn't think there was anything left to try. There was only one thing I was adamant about, after my experience with the local mental health facilities I would NEVER EVER agree to go to hospital.

4. IN HOSPITAL

Weeks later, when I had lost so much weight my clothes were hanging off me and I could no longer keep even water down it became obvious even to me that something drastic needed doing. I couldn't move without retching. I had huge black circles under my eyes from lack of sleep, and was in such a state of permanent anxiety that my body shook constantly. I could no longer hold a glass without spilling the contents everywhere. I'd tried to force myself to eat something. Convinced if I could keep anything down it would keep me out of hospital. I remember taking six dry rice crispies and trying so hard to be able to eat them. I couldn't. Every time I looked at them my stomach turned over and that dreadful acid bile would build up again.

I gave up. Gave in. Thankfully by this stage we had medical cover on our insurance, and I was able to enter one of the hospitals belonging to the Priory group.

As soon as I was registered at the desk I was shown to my room. Just like a large bedroom with an ensuite. Totally different to the day rooms I'd seen before, and nothing like the Victorian asylum picture I had in my head. It was quiet and peaceful, and I was given some time to adjust to my surroundings before the various staff members came to do their specific jobs.

I went to use the bathroom. I didn't understand how to lock the door and eventually gave up trying. I discovered later that the bathroom doors can't be locked by the patients for safety reasons. With hindsight of course not. There were many patients with many different types of mental health issues including suicidal and anorexic patients. Not to mention the majority who were on drugs that can and did lower blood pressure to the point of passing out.

I spent the first day being physically and mentally examined. I had blood tests, weight, and all the usual medical hospital observations done and was then seen by my allocated consultant psychiatrist. He asked me lots of questions I found a bit bewildering. About what day it was, who the Prime Minister was, what number came next from a sequence, and many others that should have been very easy to answer. I was very embarrassed to simply not be able to recall some of them. I felt stupid. I knew that I knew the answers, but I couldn't quite grasp them.

I know now that this is quite normal when you get into a severe depressive state, but at the time I thought it was another sign that I was literally descending into madness. This bothered me so much that during the night when I'd still been fretting about it I went to the nurse on night duty to ask if she'd let the doctor know I'd remembered who the President of America was. It is to her credit that she didn't even raise an eyebrow, said that was fine and ushered me back to bed.

For the first few days I was given little cartons of liquid meals. As I hadn't had any solid food for so long and my throat was raw with vomiting so much acid, there was no way I could face eating yet. My 'meals' were recorded and after a couple of days I was so proud to be keeping them down. To me that was a major achievement. A couple more days and I started on tiny portions of real meals (which were a bit of a shock to my stomach after so long, and caused huge bouts of pain, cramping, bloating and wind a colicky newborn would have been proud of).

I knew I was winning the food battle the day the nurse took away the liquid food chart and stopped recording every mouthful of food I managed.

During these first days I felt a bit calmer. For the first time in my life I had hope that something could and would be done to help get rid of my demons. From day one I had been put on a different anti-depressant. This time it was clomipramime. It had to be built up slowly to make sure that I could tolerate it, and to build up a resistance to the side effects. I was always very keen to show that I was doing fine and wanting increases to be done as soon as possible so I could get better and leave. However, one of the main problems was the sudden lowering of blood pressure, and I would frequently jump up from a chair or try and get out of bed too quickly, only to feel that familiar rushing sensation as the ground came up to meet me and the white stars flashed through my vision. I had to learn that some things just had to go at their own pace. I stopped asking every time I saw the consultant if I could go home yet.

As I'd been being 'weaned' back onto food, I didn't go to the dining room until I'd been there for about a week. I also hadn't gone to any of the social areas in the evenings or during breaks in the day. I'd hidden away in my room whenever I could and avoided contact with anyone as much as possible.

On my second day I had been given my own timetable. These are made up weekly and every day is planned out just like a school timetable. They are a mix of classes appropriate to your particular health issue – in my case depression, but others would have meetings for help with, for example, anorexia or addiction – as well as activities or groups where we could mix if we wanted to. For the first week I had done my recommended depression work, then scuttled off back to my room until I was expected in the therapy sessions the next day.

At the beginning of the second week however, I agreed to some additional activities so I could spend some time mixing with others on a more personal, and less structured level.

I agreed to try yoga, art therapy, and even joined a games night in the patients' room in the evening. Through this I met some amazing people who I truly admire. I had somehow supposed that having different illnesses would make us all a little wary of each other. I imagined that people would think I didn't understand, or worse didn't care as much about what they were struggling with. I had an idea of little groups set apart from each other. Addicts huddled in one corner, people with an eating disorder in another, hyper maniacs holding court in the centre and those of us with anxiety or depression trying to make ourselves invisible by the back wall.

Instead it was a very much together group. Very welcoming, caring and extremely warm and friendly. There was no hierarchy of illnesses (another myth I had convinced myself about – naturally mine would be at the bottom). I instantly regretted being too scared to leave my room for so long. I was soon in the communal kitchen where we'd make teas and coffees, grab toast and biscuits and chat in such an open and honest way as only those that know what it's like to have reached rock bottom – for whatever reason – and are all working hard on the joint struggle to climb back up. Although we didn't know all the details of each other's stories, we knew we'd all travelled our own very dark paths to get here. The feeling of fellowship and solidarity that comes with that knowledge is very powerful. We understood that we each had a painful back story, and that none of us would have chosen it, but here we all were, with all our different reasons, fighting for our mental health.

I opened up to people there in a way that I could never have done outside the hospital. As others did to me. There was the security of knowing that we were in a safe place. That everything we told each other would never go any further. And perhaps most importantly, that we would never be judged. Ironically, I felt more understanding there than I had ever experienced in my life before that, and that in itself proved to be very therapeutic.

That doesn't mean the whole stay was a bed of roses. Sometimes people would behave very strangely. Especially when they first arrived and the medication hadn't been sorted out. Whilst my way of dealing with illness was to hide away, others were the opposite. The ones coming in with high mania were the most difficult to keep calm until they'd been there long enough for treatment to start to kick in. There was one man in particular who would run off at every opportunity. Literally just stand up and run. This wouldn't have been so bad if he hadn't had a particular penchant for the pond. He made a beeline for it every time and unless he could be stopped very speedily, he always ended up jumping in. At various intervals of my stay there were shouts across the staff of "Quick, get help, Dave's in the pond again!"

Once as I was passing the nurses reception desk I was called over by a new member of staff. She was telling me how much she loved working there and had for many years, and beamed while she told me how happy she was to be back after her break. I was quite surprised to see someone so enthusiastic and who was obviously enjoying every minute of her job. That was until another member of staff came and took her gently by the arm and reminded her that as a patient she wasn't allowed on that side of the desk. The poor lady looked so disappointed. I noticed last time I was in that the desks now have to be lifted up by staff to be able to go around. I wonder if that's the reason why?

Most people I met in hospital got better, or were getting better by the time I left. I saw many different types of treatment being used while I was there. Not just medication, but the ever growing 'talking therapies', creative therapy, relaxation techniques and Electro Convulsive Therapy (ECT). This latter had to be done off site at a local hospital and whilst I was there two people were being treated. One was a woman in her thirties, and one an elderly man. I was never very sure how I felt about that. Both would be taken away on the mornings of their treatment and would be brought back again later that day but not be seen until the following day. They would then come to breakfast with one hand covered in a square white cotton padding, and none of us would ever ask about it. I am in two minds about the efficacy of this procedure. I had sat with the elderly gentleman on many evenings and he wouldn't (or couldn't?) speak a single word. He walked hunched over and never looked up. If there was a cartoon picture of 'depression' he would have been the embodiment of it. After a few sessions of ECT however, he was unrecognisable. It was like watching the sun come out. His whole posture changed. He straightened up, walked tall, laughed, actually laughed long and loud. His face would crack into a ready smile at the smallest pleasure. He was a lovely man and it was an absolute joy to see him being taken home by his family, happy and healthy and with such joy for life.

Contrarily, the woman in her thirties did not have the same positive outcome. She was manic to start with rather than depressed and would often have hallucinations, delusions, and would frequently have no idea of how she had got somewhere. She knew she was ill, but often had a great paranoia about the hospital and staff and even the patients being 'out to get her'. She had the ECT regularly, and this was still ongoing when I left, but there seemed to be no sign of her starting recovery. I have no way of knowing if it worked in the end or not. I hope so.

By the end of the fourth week I was told I was stable enough to go home, as long as I returned for regular meetings with the psychiatrist and kept up my therapy work at home. The day I left I went to the common room to say goodbye. To my surprise after railing against going to hospital for so long, and begging almost daily to be allowed home, I felt a huge sense of loss to be leaving. There were bonds there that would never be able to be made in the outside world, and people that I genuinely cared about.

There were about a dozen of my fellow boarders waiting for me. As I walked in they lined up and each one gave me a hug. It was one of the most emotional experiences of my life. The feelings of compassion and care I was given in those last minutes at the Priory have stayed with me ever since. I was quite literally overwhelmed at the time. Those wonderful people will never know how many times in the future I remembered those final moments and drew enormous strength and comfort from them. I hope that in some way each of them also received back something equally to cherish.

5. MIDDLE MOTHERHOOD

After returning home from the Priory, I couldn't wait to get back to normality as soon as possible. For me this meant trying again for a baby. However, we were told that we had to wait at least a year, partly so my body could completely recover from the miscarriage (advice I still find not wholly supported), and partly due to the amount of medication I was still on.

Although I was in much better shape than when I went into the Priory, I was also on quite strong medication, and would be for some time. So my husband and I agreed to wait the year out before trying to conceive again. I didn't want any more tablets or hormones flowing through my system than already were, so for the time being we decided condoms would be the best bet. This led to what is still one of the. Most cringeworthy experiences of my life.

We had been having problems with the heating system. After a few cold baths and no radiators working we'd called in the engineers. British Gas had been out to try and fix the boiler but with no success. A second engineer was going to be sent out with a 'missing part' and everything should be back to normal.

The engineer turned up in his little blue and white van. My husband was at work so my toddler daughter and I stayed at home for the visit. After I'd made him a cup of tea and we'd had a little chat he set to work on the dismantling and reassembling the boiler with the new piece. He'd been there about half the day by this stage and announced everything should be working now. He was just going to bleed the radiators and then wait to make sure they all heated up okay before he left.

Great, couldn't wait for that lovely hot bath and warm house. He methodically went round every downstairs radiator. Loud hissing and gurgling form each were promising signs. As he made his way up the stairs my daughter decided to follow him. It wasn't often we had visitors during the day and she was really taken with him. Actually, he'd been lovely with her, even when she'd toddled off with his screwdriver and dropped it in the fish tank.

As he went into the master bedroom, she followed him and I followed her. "Is it okay if I pull the bed out to get closer to the radiator?", he asked. "Of course, whatever's easiest". I replied before being distracted again by the little one. There was a rumble as the bed was pulled across the room followed by one of those silences that are so loud they are ear splitting. The whole atmosphere changed in an instant and I could feel dread but I had no idea why. I glanced across at the engineer to see him literally purple in the face, surrounded by dozens of empty condom wrappers which had obviously just been thrown down the. Back of the bed and had now been dislodged and floated down to the floor all around him.

We both just stood there looking first at each other, then, deeply blushing, away from each other. I have very few memories that can still cause me immense embarrassment to this day, but this is one of them. I didn't know what to do. There was nothing in my mental toolkit for dealing with this situation. I literally froze. What on earth can you say in these circumstances? Especially as the poor man was in obvious turmoil himself. He was relatively young, but even if he'd had decades of experience I doubt if he would ever have come across a similar situation, let alone know how to deal with it.

After ten years (okay, a couple of minutes), he grabbed bis toolkit, told me he needed another part from the van, ran downstairs as though his life depended on it, jumped in the van and drove off never to be seen again. He didn't even stop to check he'd not left anything behind. So, on the plus side I got to keep the screwdriver I'd rescued from the fish tank!

If that had happened now, I'd find it hysterical. If it had happened to one of my friends, I'd find it hilarious. But at that time it felt like the most embarrassing thing in the world and I was mortified for months afterwards. I was also furious with my husband who typically hadn't even been there even though he'd caused the situation. Needless to say no new wrappers were going to added to his collection for a while!

Other than this hiccup, my mental health had been improving, slowly but surely and I couldn't understand when there was a definite dip. I didn't feel as anxious as before, but my mood wasn't as good, and was quite up and down. My appetite decreased and I started to feel sick again. When I actually began to vomit again I panicked. I was on medication, a high dose. I was looking after my health, following all the recommendations I'd been given. I was still going for regular meetings with my psychiatrist. Why was I going downhill? When I started leaking small amounts of milk, although I thought it was impossible, I did a pregnancy test to make sure I wasn't pregnant before exploring other possibilities. Due to the stress my body had been though mentally and physically my periods had been very erratic since the miscarriage, so it seemed very unlikely.

It was positive! After all the angst and fuss with the bloody condoms, they hadn't worked anyway! My beautiful baby boy (as I found out later) had decided he was coming ready or not, and a plastic wrapper wasn't going to stop him.

I felt so many differing emotions as I watched the second line appear on that stick, and the time I sat there numb afterwards.

Firstly, obviously, I was shocked. Knocked sideways. We'd been so careful. Not because we didn't want another baby, but because of the advice to not conceive whilst on this medication. Then the fear came almost immediately from that thought. Oh my God! What damage could these pills be doing to my child? Had the damage already been done? If I stopped now would it be okay? Would I have caused permanent long-term damage, or would it be something mild that could be managed? As I was also very shy and always trying to follow the medical advice I'd been given, I also worried that the doctor would be cross and think I'd done it on purpose. I can't believe now that I had so little self confidence that I was worried I'd be 'told off'.

But, underneath all of that was a small, bubbling feeling of elation. It was one of many mixed emotions, but it was there. With everything that was going on in my body and mind, my baby had decided the time was right no matter what I or anyone else said, and he was growing solidly inside me, giving me a special joy and every day I loved him a little bit more.

There followed some rapidly booked appointments with doctors, midwives and my psychiatrist. Yes, the medication had to be stopped immediately. It's dangerous to cut it out instantly, but it was cut down and out very quickly. The psychiatrist had said not to worry, the pregnancy hormones would kick in and give me the 'lift' I needed to replace the meds and avoid depression. He was talking crap. The 'lift' was nothing compared to coming down from such a high dose of chemicals, and I was obviously now going through withdrawal at the same time. There was the added worry that there was not enough previous research done to show whether or not the baby would have any damage already done, and it was going to be a case of hoping I'd stopped the meds in time, but basically we'd just have to wait and see.

My psychiatrist could see I was going to spiral downwards, particularly after the birth when what he called the 'happy hormones' disappeared, and was obviously keen to pass the problem on. He suggested I be referred to a female psychologist who specialised in pre and post natal depression. This was a fairly new specialisation then, and there was one clinic available relatively near, and only be recommendation from a previous consultant. I was lucky enough to be accepted by this new team, and even more lucky that the new psychiatrist was outstanding in her dealings with patients and her up to date knowledge of psychological problems associated with, or exacerbated by, pregnancy.

She knew what was coming for me. Fortunately, I didn't. I struggled through this pregnancy with none of the highs I'd experienced during my first. The birth was more straightforward. I was overdue again, but this time instead of being two weeks late and needing my waters broken, it was just over a week after the due date that I woke up to find I'd wet the bed. I jumped out of bed in surprise, wondering how on earth I could have had a wee without noticing and saw water was running down my legs. Not wee. I woke my husband and he too jumped out of bed. And asked me to please stop weeing on the carpet. I pointed out (relatively politely) that no I couldn't, it wasn't wee and I had absolutely no control over it. He disappeared for a minute and I assumed he'd gone to ring the hospital. No, he reappeared with a huge towel for me to stand on and then he rang the hospital while I stood in a large puddle with a bemused look on my face.

We squelched our way to hospital (well I squelched). I had no idea you lost so much water. The first time I'd been lying down and not seen the amount that came out. This time it was like having a little tap permanently on. I continued squelching through the hospital corridors until we arrived at maternity and I was examined, told to wait until they decided where I was to be put – not sent home due to waters breaking and risk of infection, but not in the labour ward as they thought there would be at least another 24 hours. We sat around chatting for a number of hours before I was eventually put in a general ward. As I'd been up since early that morning with my waters breaking at dawn, and had spent the day waiting around, I was really tired by the time I was allocated a bed. A kind nurse gave me a mild sedative so I could get a 'good night's sleep before going into labour probably tomorrow night'.

Three hours later I was fighting the sedatives effects, while sucking on gas and air and giving birth to my amazing little boy.

Twenty minutes after that both me and my son were out for the count due to birth, sedatives and gas and air.

My husband was left on his own having been called in time to be at the birth, now sitting dumbstruck after the speed of everything in the middle of the night, looking at his wife and child, neither of whom stirred until morning.

Fortunately, my son had no ill effects from the medication I'd been on at the beginning of my pregnancy, and was a happy, healthy, absolute bundle of joy. Unfortunately, as expected, and as I'd been forewarned, there was a very rapid deterioration in my mental health after the birth. There was a new drug I'd agreed to try that had been discussed in advance, but it wasn't suitable for use during pregnancy or breast feeding. I'd breast fed my first child for over a year, and wanted to do the same for this one, but had agreed that when the balance of my mental health deteriorating outweighed the benefits of my continuing feeding I'd switch to bottles and start medication.

I tried so hard to keep going for as long as possible. Every day I became increasingly subdued. Yet every day I felt I was doing the best for my son and didn't want to feel I'd failed at yet another thing. So the inward battle raged on. I know breastfeeding isn't for everyone. And I strongly believe it is each individual's choice. But this was one of the few things I thought I could do for my children, and there was plenty that I thought I was incapable of. So for my own sense of achievement, this mattered. By the middle of the second month, however, I couldn't get out of bed. My baby was brought to me for feeding, but I had become unable once again to stomach food myself. By three months I was back to the old, now familiar routines of vomiting, shaking, palpitations, difficulty breathing and swallowing, my throat bleeding again due to constantly being dry and sick, and the absolute rolling terrors again happening without relief. So, one again I had to give in and keep my promise to the new psychiatrist.

She was brilliant. There was no judgement about how much I'd let myself go down before returning to see her. Just genuine help and caring. We had our longest talk ever. Now pregnancy wasn't an issue, she wanted to ensure I was on the correct medication that would stabilise me quickly and keep that stability maintained in the future.

We went through dozens of questions, in real depth. At the end she asked what my diagnosis was. "Clinical depression and acute anxiety", I told her. I've apparently been suffering it for over a decade.

"Hmmm...has anyone ever mentioned that you may be bi-polar?"

"No. Never. Absolutely not. I am definitely not bi-polar in the slightest".

"I think you're bi-polar."

No way. That's a serious mental illness. People with manic depression are really nuts! Do strange things. Don't always act normally. Can be irrational. Irritable. Moody. Lots of other things...that I sometimes am...and more...

Oh.

6. BACK A BIT

Bipolar Disorder? Really? Hmmm...not too sure about that. But...thinking back...a lot of things would make sense.

I had always been a painfully shy child. I was very small and felt permanently awkward and embarrassed. I was very anxious in most situations, yet would think nothing of jumping off sheds and garages to see how far away I could land. I was terrified of being lost, but would go for walks for miles without telling anyone or knowing where I was going. I did this from about aged five or six and used to sneak out of the house to go and find an adventure (too many Enid Blyton books!). I would take breadcrumbs to leave a trail. (Ok I know NOW that was stupid).

I'd walk through fields for hours looking for tunnels into the ground, only worrying when it got dark and I had no idea where I was. Once a neighbour found me and brought me home, but usually I just wandered about until I saw something I recognised and then made my own way home. We lived in a bungalow in a quiet area for a lot of my childhood, so getting in and out of the window for my secret escapes was rarely an issue.

From being a very small child, my sleep was never regular. Even when I was at school with a steady routine I would be up half the night. When I was young I would just stay in my room and read and nobody would know. As I got older, I would get up and do things around the house, often until dawn. I would manage quite easily during these phases with just a few hours sleep. Then frequently crash at the weekend and sleep for twenty four or thirty six hours straight. This pattern continued when I started work. No matter how hard I tried to have a 'normal' routine, it just wouldn't happen.

I also hated school. I didn't fit in, possibly due to feeling so different from everyone else. I tried every trick in the book to get out of school, constantly complaining of stomach aches and head aches. At secondary school, when I was no longer actually taken, I often left in the morning, doubled back and returned home when everyone else had left. This backfired on more than one occasion when I re-entered the house only to realise someone was still in, due to a day off for holiday or illness, or some other reason. I have spent whole days hiding in either a cupboard, or behind the sofa rather than be discovered inside and sent back to school.

Looking back, I must have driven my poor siblings nuts! I wold beg them to stay up with me, and when they didn't – because, being like most people, needing to actually have sufficient sleep at night – I would wake them with 'surprises' that they couldn't refuse. I cooked my poor sister a three course meal one night. She was woken at three o'clock in the morning by me bearing a tray with a full roast dinner on it! I'd started at midnight and made a trifle to go with it as that was her favourite. I can still picture her face when I woke her up. I thought she'd be delighted, but naturally she was totally bewildered and more than a little confused – partly due to what I was doing and partly due to being still half asleep.

I thought nothing of disturbing her night as I genuinely thought she'd be pleased. The only thing that bothered me was that the jelly in the trifle hadn't had time to set properly and I was worried that would spoil the meal. She tells me now that I regularly did things like that, but she gradually became so used to them it didn't really matter anymore, and she learned to expect the unexpected. In my defence I was always well intentioned and spent a long time thinking about things to do that I thought would please others.

I would buy paint, and overnight completely change the colour of a room. Or spend three days wallpapering non-stop and then collapse into sleep for days.

Some of my ideas were just bizarre. (Easy to say with hindsight). Once my parents had been complaining the carpet looked old and needed replacing. I had read somewhere about natural ways to maintain and clean a house, and knew there had been a tip about making carpets like new, but couldn't remember the exact details. This was long before anything like Google. All I could remember was that using things found in nature was the basis of the idea and I had a feeling had been straw was involved.

Not unsurprisingly, we didn't have any straw available. I remembered my father had mown the grass the day before, but not collected up the clippings. I wasn't in school that day. So, once everyone else had left that morning for school or work, and the house was empty, I started work.

I collected armfuls of cut, damp, grass, and spread them all over the living room carpet until it was completely covered. Quite literally covered. There was no sign at all of the carpet beneath. I then stamped across it over and over again to trample the grass in, which was supposed to attract the dirt to it so it could all be easily removed afterwards along with the grass.

This whole process took hours. I was very pleased with myself at the end. I was sure the carpet would look like new and the room would smell fresh and clean, and my parents would be delighted.

This didn't happen. Firstly, the grass was damp, and my trampling over it had just made it worse. Instead of the swift brushing out of the room I'd envisaged, leaving a spotless carpet, I couldn't even sweep it up. Every time I tried, pieces of grass rolled into balls, chunks of it stuck to the broom, and none of it would actually form any sort of pile that I could pick up to remove. Eventually I had to resort to picking it up by hand. (Taking it back outside as there was far too much to put in the bin, ironically leaving it in a very similar position in the garden to where I'd started that morning).

Secondly, once I'd removed most of the grass, I had intended to just run a vacuum over the floor to finish off. However, there were so many small, sticky, pieces of grass left, that within minutes I'd broken the Hoover. The wet remains stuck to the Hoover's brushes and completely clogged the mechanism. I tried very ineffectively to pull them out, but they were all in tangled, knotted clumps. I tried desperately to clean up somehow. By now my siblings were back from school, gleefully pronouncing that my parents would be home soon and were going to kill me.

I had a last ditch attempt with a hand brush, but even I had to admit defeat. By the time my parents walked in I had been working for a solid nine hours, and the room looked (and smelled) like a tip. There was still grass all over the place, now drying and stinking the whole house out. The smell was rotten and damp, and the floor was worse. No longer was there even a chance of saving the old carpet, never mind cleaning it. Added to the original problems, it was now damp, smelly and had some new and very strange stains on it. Needless to say, my parents were not happy with me, and even less so when I tried to explain exactly what I'd done. At that stage I'm not sure whether they thought I was mad or bad.

I do know that they then suggested that if I wanted to help, I could just stick to making meals. Fine by me, but they were always going to be made in my own inimitable way.

I made good, nutritious meals, from scratch. But there would always be something different about them, simply because I would get bored so easily. I used a lot of food dye. Potatoes for example would usually be blue, or green if I thought that matched the rest of the meal better. Scrambled eggs could be red to 'brighten' a meal up. Sometimes I would make rainbow colours of everything on the plate.

I even managed to make luminous chops once when I braised them in a mixture of spices. That was a one off as I've still no idea how I managed it, but it was certainly a talking point!

My family got used to the idea of ignoring the look and colour of whatever I'd made and just eating it. It tasted fine, and after a while I don't think they really noticed anymore. Fortunately, by the time I moved out, married and had a family of my own, I was bored with colouring in food so didn't continue this (much) in my grown-up life.

In fact, I've always made a supreme effort to be as normal as possible when I had my children. I'd ask myself before embarking on anything, how many people I knew would do this, and if the answer was none, I'd give whatever master plan I'd just had a wide berth! I thought I'd done quite well over the years, but every now and then I'm caught by a comment from one of my children. For example, when offering to take one of them shopping with a friend the answer was an adamant, "Not with my friends, Mum, it's embarrassing when you dance in the shop." Shit. I thought I hadn't done that for years.

My eldest, now grown up, has however admitted that their friends always thought I was a cool Mum. Apparently, this was because I always joined in with their games, no matter how childish. I also gave some great Birthday parties because one thing about bipolar is if you're going to put effort into something you go all out with it. I have done many weird and wonderful children's parties over the years, and happily dressed like a witch or similar for a special theme. I've made use of my earlier acquired food colouring skills for amazing, unique party food, and generally made a complete fool of myself for the sole benefit of keeping my children happy. Apparently, nobody else's mother is as mad as me.

I'll take that as a compliment. These are few and far between when you've spent your life fighting and trying to hide mental illness.

7. KILL OR CURE

The answer to depression – bipolar or otherwise – has for many years revolved around medication. Consideration has only been given to talking therapies relatively recently, and these tend to be given in conjunction with medication, or other therapies (such as Electro-Convulsive Therapy – (ECT)).

You don't have to look too far back in history to see the inhumanity in the ways in which people with mental illnesses used to be treated. The lunatic asylums even of the relatively modern post Victorian era rightly cause shudders when mentioned, and the overriding abhorrence of 'treatments' given, and punishments used on those already suffering often unbearable illness is not to be underestimated.

From being starved, stripped, beaten and isolated in the name of looking after those unsuitable to be out in the Community because of a mental illness - often not even a genuine medical issue, but due to, for example, family wanting rid of a pregnant adolescent daughter, or 'hysterical' women, who in reality were often deeply traumatised being sent for a 'cure' and who often remained in these places until the end of their lives.

To being guinea pigs for the progressive new ideas on how modern medicine could transform a person back to 'normality' by using drastic surgery such as lobotomies. The person being operated on in such a manner not even being able to refuse consent because, "They're mad...we don't need their consent. We can do what we like as long as it's in the patient's best interests. And of course it is...we think...worth a try anyway." The absolute power of those medics was truly frightening, but not as much as the total lack of any advocacy for the patients.

Imagine having the audacity to argue against the terror of being put forward for these procedures and fighting back only to be put in a strait jacket and locked in a cell like room. Proving beyond doubt to those in charge that you were indeed insane. The cruelty these people endured at the hands of 'professionals' seems barbaric.

It would be nice to think that we have come such a long way in a relatively short period of time to have moved from surgery to medication, but is it really that much more advanced?

Of course, the medications currently used are constantly being improved and modernised. We've come a long way from the 'one size fits all' attitude as well. But

they are certainly not an easy answer.
Unfortunately for some people they are the
only answer at the moment. But it can be a
choice a lot of us are very reluctant to take.
Sometimes the hoped for benefits are almost
outweighed by the possible – often probable
– side effects. These can be horrendous,
varying from slight nausea to death, with
everything in between.

I have been on many different tablets over
the last three decades. Some haven't
worked at all. Others have been effective for
a while but then had to be stopped either
because they simply stopped working, or

because the side effects became too much to be able to function with, or too dangerous.

I have been on so many different types of tablets that there is no way I could possibly remember them all. Going through my old cupboards I have however found the remaining packaging/pills of the following list. Some are anti-anxiety, others, antidepressants, and a few to supplement these to try and stop palpitations/nausea caused by the former. These are by no means all I have been tried on, but they give a good idea of the poisons that have been a necessary part of my life for so long.

In no particular order (i.e. the way they came out of the drawers and cupboards!):

Pregablin, Lamotrigine, Priadel (Lithium), Verapamil, Olanzapine, Vortioxetine, Quetiapine, Sertraline, Diazepam, Agomelatine, Mirtazepine (Zispin), Fluoxetine, Lorazepam, Clomipramine (Anafranil), Nortriptyline (Motipress), Gabapentin, Venlafaxine...

These all have the possibility of some very severe side effects, including (this is by no means even close to an exhaustive list) the following:

Nausea, vomiting, hypertension (high blood pressure), hypotension (low blood pressure), changes in libido, lactation (producing milk), memory loss, pseudoparkinsonism, shaking, dizziness, tremors, dystonia (prolonged abnormal muscle spasms), gastritis, loss of appetite, salivation, excessive perspiration, dry mouth, headache, constipation, blurred vision, tachycardia, glaucoma, bladder paralysis, faecal impaction, weight change, menstrual irregularities, skin problems including itching, eczema, dermatitis, and photosensitivity, many types of blood disorders, kidney and liver damage, psychotic flare ups, increased risk of suicide, serotonin syndrome, hallucinations, heart problems including arrhythmia, even cancers and sudden death...you get the idea.

I have suffered many of these side effects. Physically the worst for me were the mini explosion type bangs in my head – which were genuinely terrifying - and the heart problems, at one stage my circulation became so bad my legs were blue. Mentally the most difficult were the huge weight gain and the lactation. To start a certain medication and quickly not be able to fit into any of your clothes or look in a mirror and see someone you hardly recognise is very difficult. And to be producing milk when not pregnant or having a baby I found very disturbing.

A further complication to finding the right solution is that it takes four to six weeks for a new medication to take effect. There is unfortunately no 'magic pill'. (Which I firmly believed there would be the first time I was hospitalized, and was very disappointed to find this wasn't the case). This means that there is a long 'wait and see' period. Sometimes you have to fight through the side effects for weeks hoping they'll ease enough to be able to function (often in my case severe bouts of daily vomiting), only to find the medication either ineffective or too toxic for my body to handle.

This leads to the nightmare of having to withdraw from one medication slowly (the side effects of withdrawal can sometimes be very severe), then often having to leave a couple of weeks gap before starting a new trial as the medicines can often interact with each other. During this withdrawal and restart time I would be acutely aware that there was nothing going into my body that could even have a chance of shifting the depression. These were some of the toughest times as at least when I was building medication strengths up, I could convince myself that this time it would work. When I was changing or coming off medication, I often felt that this would be the time I couldn't get better and it was sheer bloodymindedness that kept me going.

I hate taking any type of tablets. I loathe what they do to my body, both inside and out. But unfortunately, I appear to have no choice. If I stop completely, I will eventually just grind to a halt. My brain will no longer function. I will gradually become unable to think properly, communicate effectively or manage basic everyday tasks – like getting out of bed. My body will quickly follow suit and I will stop eating, start vomiting and become physically incapable of doing almost anything.

As I get older, I become less tolerant of toxins going into my body, but also have more severe and longer lasting bouts of depression when they occur. This makes finding effective treatment more complicated. Sometimes it's a case of mix and match one or two drugs, at other times it seems to be a kill or cure gamble.

To go back to those asylums mentioned above. Am I glad I didn't live then, when that would have been my only likely outcome? Of course. But to live in the future where hopefully treatment is different and other ways are found to manage depression successfully would be even better!

Imagine a world where depression is something eased quickly and completely. One 'magic pill' and it's gone. Or even better, a vaccination so no-one has to ever know the pain it causes. And maybe future generations looking back at now and shaking their heads at how barbaric treatment still was in 2020, with your choices being to take your chances being filled with toxins or strapped into a chair for your weekly ECT session. Or both.

At least I would never have to endure the indignity and trauma of putting myself through ECT...

8. ECT

I agreed to the ECT. I was so ill by then I think I would have agreed to a lobotomy.

Even though I thought this was my last chance of anything working, I was absolutely terrified. Not of the ECT itself, but of the anaesthetic. I'd had a fear of being 'put to sleep' since as a child I had needed seven (baby) teeth taking out at once due to the position they were growing in. This was done under a general anaesthetic and I have vivid memories of waking up afterwards leaning over a sink with my mouth pouring blood and switching from sleep to panic within seconds. This obviously wasn't helped by not being able to eat solid food for days and being in a lot of pain. I was left with a deep fear of ever needing another general.

By the night before I'd worked myself up into a right state. As the Priory aren't allowed to do the procedure on their premises – it has to be done is a clinical hospital setting in case of any problems or medical issues arising – I had to go to a nearby hospital.

I wasn't getting much sleep anyway due to the depression and anxiety levels, but that night I didn't sleep at all. The nurse came in to do a MMSE (mini mental state examination). This is used to measure levels of memory and cognition. It is often used by doctors to spot the initial stages of dementia before a referral is made for further testing. They were checking my short term memory and would do so the evening before every treatment. Simple questions about current affairs, for example, who is the Prime Minister? Followed by a sequence of simple instructions such as first, fold this paper, then put it on the floor. Finished with trying to recall a road address that had been given to me a few minutes earlier. It sounds easy. It is easy. And I had no problems during this stay in hospital. But it reminded me so clearly of the first time I'd been admitted and I was in such a deep depression and so sleep deprived that I couldn't even remember the name of the then Prime Minister.

I took my evening meds and then watched the ceiling until dawn.

I was due to get a taxi from the Priory to the hospital. I wasn't allowed to eat or drink beforehand and I was dressed and ready about two hours before we were due to leave (I had to be chaperoned). As the hospital were expecting us at 9am we had to leave at 8am to allow for traffic on the forty minute journey.

I sat trying to quell the rising panic and accompanying nausea. Trying to think of anything to distract myself. Couldn't even have a glass of water to sip.

Shortly before 8am the nurse who was coming with me took me took the foyer and we sat and waited for the taxi to pull up.

I can't explain the sheer terror I felt waiting there. I was shaking uncontrollably and trying to pretend I was fine. I didn't want to talk about it. I'd been through all the catastrophising scenarios in my head on loop. Now I just needed to get it over with. My adrenalin and heart rate were through the roof. So we waited.

An hour later we were still waiting. The nurse went to try and find out what was going on. When she returned, I knew by her face it wasn't good news.

"I'm so sorry about this". She genuinely meant it. "The hospital had a mix up and didn't have you down for today, which is why nobody has been sent to pick you up. They're booking you in for Tuesday instead."

She was kind. "At least you can eat something now. How about I organise some toast for you and a cup of tea?"

I couldn't handle it. All the fear I'd been fighting erupted. I ran sobbing back to my room and threw up all the bile in my stomach.

Incredibly this scene was repeated the following Tuesday. But this time it was supposedly down to a technical problem and I was assured I hadn't been forgotten.

Third time lucky! We repeated the now familiar evening routine with the MMSE, were waiting at 8am, and I was more than a little surprised to see the taxi pulling up. I had been a bit calmer this time. Perhaps subconsciously I thought it was never going to happen. But as we got into the taxi the panic attack started. I couldn't breathe. I certainly couldn't bear any of the inane chit chat that was supposed to take my mind off it. I focused on a spot in the distance. Took deep breaths in between the shallow panting ones and clenched my fist around the plastic bag in my pocket that I still carried everywhere with me in case of violently throwing up without warning.

Wave after wave of panic engulfed me on that journey. It is difficult to explain to someone who hasn't experienced it that it doesn't really just ease off. It's like a perpetual onslaught with no reason to it. There are techniques that can be learnt to help, but at the time I was way beyond being able to access them.

When we arrived there was a lot of whispering between the nurse who was chaperoning me and the desk staff at the main reception. I felt like an exhibit from the zoo. I'm sure they didn't mean to stare so openly but it was bloody obvious. I've often thought I should hold a sign or wear a badge saying 'Yes, I'm mad', to answer the politely unasked – but blatantly obvious - questions. I may be nuts, but I'm not deaf or blind. I can actually see the raised eyebrows, the flicker of interest before risking a shooting glance to see what mad people actually look like. I can also tell when you're talking about me. You can say my name quietly, and whisper the word bi-polar, but please don't assume I'm not aware you're talking about me. Again, mad – not stupid.

After I'd been checked in, we were led through a clinic door and down a long corridor. We then took a lift which opened near a waiting room. This first time, it was empty, and I didn't have to wait long before I was called into the 'operating room'. I'm not really sure what to call it. It wasn't at all like a traditional theatre. For a start there was no big bed. I'm not sure what I was expecting, but at the very least a huge antiquated theatre bed, covered in straps and ties to bind you down with. In fact, if this doesn't sound daft, I was quite pleasantly surprised.

There were a few staff surrounding what was more like a large reclined chair than a bed. No bondage – thank God for that! Yes, there were a couple of small straps for my arms (and I think for my legs, but as I was in more of a sitting position and definitely not staring at my legs I can't totally recall). Of course, it is possible that once I was asleep there were more, but not that I'm aware of.

When I'd been at the dental hospital as a child I'd remembered this huge mask clamped over my face and I'd been dreading that, but that never happened here. I had an injection in the back of my hand with smiling staff watching me as I drifted into unconsciousness. I can't remember how many were in there, perhaps four or five? And I can't remember any of their faces. But I do remember feeling that they were kindly and well meaning. Unlike the bloody dentist who had the bedside manner of Attila the Hun!

I have no idea how long the actual ECT treatment took (obviously), but apparently it's only minutes. I woke up to find the needle out of my hand, replaced with a neat cotton square. Actually I know that's what happened as the padding was there when I arrived back at the Priory, but I don't actually remember anything from being put to sleep until later that evening. I don't recall leaving the hospital (probably had even more weird looks now I had my 'padded hand'), or the taxi back, or whether/when I ate or drank. I felt okay afterwards. And although I continued to worry more about the general than the treatment on future visits, I wasn't as anxious about going as I had initially been.

If there are any medical practitioners reading this, perhaps it may be an idea to discuss this with the patient beforehand. Yes, the procedure was explained to me, but not the setting. It would have eased a fair bit of anxiety to know the environment I was going into was not at all the dungeon of gloom I'd imagined. To know the 'theatre' was not an enormous clinical stainless steel cell (which is what I'd imagined), and just the general reality of what I was going to see and what was going to happen. It really could make a difference to future patients.

The second visit followed a similar pattern. By the third I'd stopped worrying about whoever was on reception and what they thought of me, and the anaesthetist had realised I was panicking due to being knocked out and started to put the injection in immediately I was seated in the correct position rather than having any small talk first. Previously we had both watched the machines showing a very quick raise in my heart rate and blood pressure the longer I had to wait and worry.

On a couple of occasions there were one or two other people in the ECT waiting room. I remember a very sad looking woman who didn't speak at all, but looked so mournful I just wanted to put my arms around her. And a man who was the total opposite. He was talking non-stop. Very hyper and manic. He told me he'd been for lots of ECT on many occasions and he actually seemed quite happy about it. He was full of questions and yet away in his own little world. I quite liked him. It's strange but most people would probably have run a mile, whereas I felt an affinity with him. Okay we were both about to have our heads fried (I can say that, we did it), but we both had that immediate link. We had something in common that, let's be honest, not many people are going to relate to. I often wonder now what happened to him. I hope he's okay and in a good mental place.

After the third treatment I had a bad headache that gradually worsened. It took a couple of days to go completely. After the fourth treatment the same happened and this time there was a large throbbing pain behind my left eye. As I was still in the Priory we discussed the pros and cons of continuing treatment. There hadn't been a noticeable mood improvement but it had been explained it could take six or nine sessions for this to happen. We decided to continue, but unfortunately the pain was so bad after the fifth treatment, and continued for so long, that I was genuinely worried I may be doing some permanent damage, and so it was stopped.

Back to the drawing board.

Back to medication.

At the beginning of last year, I was on one of the biggest cocktails of drugs I've had to have. Every day I was taking 800mg Lithium, 75mg Pregablin, 50mg Agomelatine, and 250mg Sertraline. Added to this were one to three Metroclomopromide tablets to take as necessary to stop me throwing up all the others! (As well Bisoprolol every evening due to my erratic heartbeat).

It was almost impossible to have any type of normality due to feeling like I was drowning in medication. The tiredness and nausea were awful – but not nearly as bad as the depression so I persevered for as long as possible before lowering some of the doses.

It's a constant balancing act. I have cut down as much as possible, but I am aware that there will come a point when my brain requires some stimulation I just cannot seem to produce naturally.

And so, I will continue as best I can, hopeful of that elusive miracle cure one day becoming a reality.

9. ...AND FINALLY

I've obviously struggled with Bipolar disorder all my life, even though I wasn't diagnosed until my late thirties. Being given a definitive diagnosis may have helped the health professionals, but I don't think it made a great difference to me.

'Celebrities' who have declared they have similar illnesses are often heard saying that although periods in their lives can be hard, they wouldn't change their illness. They would keep their condition if given a choice. This is probably because they have become very successful, and perhaps the good outweighs the bad.

Given the choice I would get rid of this disease like a shot. It has dogged my entire life and feels like a permanent weight on my shoulders.

But I haven't been given a choice. I just have to get on with it. I try to be thankful that I have still managed to have a loving family and live a relatively 'normal' life. Albeit with regular visits to doctors and trips to hospitals. Even a few generations ago that may not have been possible.

I can't change what I have, no matter how much I want to, so I will live the best way I can.

I've written this all down in the hope that it can give some hope to both those suffering with Bipolar disorder, and those who care about them. To show there is still a positive and productive life possible. It just takes more effort!

For family and friends, it can be tough seeing someone you love spiralling downwards and not being able to do anything about it. But just being there is enough.

Life may be really difficult at times, but these times WILL pass.

My own mantra has kept me going over the years. Sometimes I just have it on repeat in my head all throughout the lowest points, and it keeps me going until the next lot of tablets kick in: *Everything is transient.* Hold onto that thought. Be kind to yourself.
